W9-DHU-170

RACIAL JUSTICE IN AMERICA
EXCELLENCE AND ACHIEVEMENT

HISTORICALLY BLACK COLLEGES and UNIVERSITIES

KELISA WING

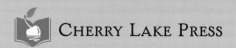
CHERRY LAKE PRESS

Published in the United States of America by Cherry Lake Publishing Group
Ann Arbor, Michigan
www.cherrylakepublishing.com

Reading Adviser: Beth Walker Gambro, MS, Ed., Reading Consultant, Yorkville, IL
Content Adviser: Kelisa Wing
Book Design and Cover Art: Felicia Macheske

Photo Credits: Library of Congress, Photo by Frances Benjamin Johnston, LOC Control No: 2017650161, 5; © Eric Glenn/Shutterstock.com, 7; © ARK NEYMAN/Shutterstock.com, 9; © Robert Clay/Alamy Stock Photo, 10; Library of Congress, Brady-Handy photograph collection, LOC Control No: 2017896545, 13; © ZUMA Press, Inc./Alamy Stock Photo, 14, 18; © Cubankite/Shutterstock.com, 17; © Nuno21/Shutterstock.com, 21; © REUTERS/Alamy Stock Photo, 22; © SDI Productions/iStock.com, 25; Library of Congress, Harris & Ewing, photographer, LOC Control No: 2016877613, 26; © Tverdokhlib/Shutterstock.com, 29; © Conner Flecks/Alamy Stock Photo, 30;

Graphics Throughout: © debra hughes/Shutterstock.com; © Galyna_P/Shutterstock.com

Copyright © 2022 by Cherry Lake Publishing Group

All rights reserved. No part of this book may be reproduced or utilized in any form or by any means without written permission from the publisher.

Cherry Lake Press is an imprint of Cherry Lake Publishing Group.

Library of Congress Cataloging-in-Publication Data

Names: Wing, Kelisa, author.
Title: Historically black colleges and universities / by Kelisa Wing.
Description: Ann Arbor, Michigan : Cherry Lake Publishing, [2022] | Series: Racial justice in America: excellence and achievement | Audience: Grades 7-9 | Summary: "Readers will learn more about the history, traditions, and modern achievements of Historically Black Colleges and Universities (HBCUs). From Howard University and homecoming celebrations to all the amazing graduates of HBCUs, students will discover what makes these institutions so special and vital to America. The Racial Justice in America: Excellence and Achievement series celebrates Black achievement and culture, while exploring racism in a comprehensive, honest, and age-appropriate way. Developed in conjunction with educator, advocate, and author Kelisa Wing to reach children of all races and encourage them to approach our history with open eyes and minds. Books include 21st Century Skills and content, activities created by Wing, table of contents, glossary, index, author biography, sidebars, and educational matter"—Provided by publisher.
Identifiers: LCCN 2021047042 | ISBN 9781534199293 (hardcover) | ISBN 9781668900437 (paperback) | ISBN 9781668901878 (pdf) | ISBN 9781668906194 (ebook)
Subjects: LCSH: African American universities and colleges—History—Juvenile literature. | African Americans—Education—History—Juvenile literature. | African Americans—Education—Social aspects—Juvenile literature. | Racism in education—United States—History—Juvenile literature.
Classification: LCC LC2781 .W564 2022 | DDC 378.1/982996073—dc23/eng/20211006
LC record available at https://lccn.loc.gov/2021047042

Cherry Lake Publishing Group would like to acknowledge the work of the Partnership for 21st Century Learning, a Network of Battelle for Kids. Please visit *http://www.battelleforkids.org/networks/p21* for more information.

Printed in the United States of America
Corporate Graphics

All glory to God. For Naima and Jadon and all of our babies! Success is having joy, getting up each day and doing what you love, and being unapologetically who you were created to be. Thank you, Donald, for your liberatory love.

Kelisa Wing honorably served in the U.S. Army and has been an educator for 14 years. She is the author of *Promises and Possibilities: Dismantling the School to Prison Pipeline, If I Could: Lessons for Navigating an Unjust World*, and *Weeds & Seeds: How to Stay Positive in the Midst of Life's Storms*. She speaks both nationally and internationally about discipline reform, equity, and student engagement. Kelisa lives in Northern Virginia with her husband and two children.

CHAPTER 1

What Are HBCUs?

"What do you want to do when you grow up?"

You've probably been asked that question over and over again. Some students dream of becoming a doctor, a lawyer, a politician, or even president of the United States. Some students want to learn a trade and join the workforce after they graduate from school. For many students, to do what they dream of becoming as an adult requires them to first attend college. What college to attend is something many students think about, especially as they get older. But what if you could not be what you wanted to be or go to college because of the color of your skin? For Black students before the Civil Rights Act was signed into law, this was a reality.

For a very long time in America, Black students were not able to attend colleges or universities with White students.

Historically Black Colleges and Universities (HBCUs) are an important part of American life, history, and culture. These colleges and universities historically served Black people and provided a way for them to get an education when they could not go to other colleges and universities. Out of the 5,300 colleges and universities in the United States, only 107 are HBCUs. While the number of HBCUs may be small, their impact is significant. Although HBCUs were created to educate Black people, any person can attend them.

HBCUs have become more popular in the last year. The murder of George Floyd and the protests of summer 2020 created an increase in applications to HBCUs.

CHAPTER 2

The History of HBCUs

Long before slavery was abolished, some states passed anti-literacy laws. These laws banned enslaved people and free Black men and women from learning how to read or write. They also made it illegal for other people to teach them.

White people enacted anti-literacy laws because they were afraid of enslaved people becoming educated and rising up against the horrible system of slavery. Even though it was illegal to learn how to read and write, many enslaved people still did all they could to become literate. One such person was Frederick Douglass. He was taught the alphabet as a young boy and started trading food to learn even more from other children. Through reading and writing, he escaped a life of slavery. Douglass wrote *The Narrative of the Life of Frederick Douglass* and became one of the most famous abolitionists.

How does knowing how to read and write empower a person?

About 600 students attend Cheyney University.

Understanding the power of literacy, Richard Humphreys established the African Institute in 1837 in Pennsylvania. This is the first HBCU and is now called Cheyney University. Many Black people were still enslaved during this time. Humphreys wanted to create a way for freed men and women to learn how to read, write, and gain skills to help them as they started their lives as free people.

Richard Humphreys was born in the West Indies. He vowed to create a school for people of African descent that would prepare them for life beyond slavery. He also gave money to a shelter for Black orphans and three clinics that provided care for Black patients. He saw a need and did something about it.

In 1823, Alexander Twilight became the first Black person to graduate from college. After his accomplishment, nearly 40 Black people attended college in the North before the end of the Civil War. The Emancipation Proclamation was signed in 1863 and was fully enacted in 1865. Black people had attended colleges and universities, but they weren't always treated kindly and were sometimes made to feel unwelcome.

In 1890, the Second Morrill Act was proposed by Senator Justin Smith Morrill and passed by the U.S. Congress. This law said that Black people had to be included in the U.S. higher education system. This included states that had separate colleges for Black and White students. It required those states to create colleges that would provide Black students with skills and career opportunities in agriculture, mechanics, and architecture. As a result of this act, 19 HBCUs and 33 tribal universities were built, providing many people with an education.

Senator Morrill knew the importance of educated citizens, regardless of race or background.

The marching band at South Carolina State is known as the Marching 101.
They're one of the best marching bands in the country.

Fraternities and sororities are an important part of HBCUs. The National Pan-Hellenic Council (NPHC) was founded at Howard University as a way to unite Black fraternities and sororities. The NPHC has nine fraternities and sororities called "The Divine Nine."

HBCUs are also known for their homecoming events in the fall months. Homecoming is a time for current and former students to celebrate their pride in their HBCU. The events feature food, dancing, parades, sports, and fraternity and sorority step shows. Stepping is a type of dance that uses voice, stomps, steps, and claps to create a complicated rhythm.

CHAPTER 3

Famous People Who Attended HBCUs

Oprah Winfrey graduated from high school in 1972. She attended Tennessee State University and left school to become the first Black news anchor in Nashville. She was one credit short of receiving her degree but went back to school in 1986 to finish her last credit and graduate.

Winfrey chose the university because of the journalism program they offered. She also got a full scholarship. Many HBCUs give scholarships to promising students each year.

Oprah Winfrey donates regularly to HBCUs including Morehouse College and Tennessee State University. She has also donated money to the United Negro College Fund.

Strahan was inducted to the Pro Football Hall of Fame in 2014.

Michael Strahan attended Texas Southern University, where he played football. Strahan then played defensive lineman in the NFL for the New York Giants. He grew up living all over the world and even attended school in Germany. He said his HBCU experience made him feel like he belonged.

Strahan is now a cohost of *Good Morning America*. Many people who attend HBCUs remember all the opportunities they had as a result of attending there. From sports to clubs to student organizations, there are many benefits to going to an HBCU.

Martin Luther King Jr. attended Morehouse College in Atlanta, Georgia. Morehouse is a school for men. King was part of the debate team, glee club, and student council during his time there. He learned a lot about nonviolence and wrote many famous papers while there. He graduated in 1948 and used what he learned as a leader of the civil rights movement. Many other students learn about advocacy at HBCUs.

Kamala Devi Harris attended Howard University in Washington, D.C. Howard University was established in 1867 and focuses on programs for liberal arts and medicine. Harris is the first woman and first South Asian American and Black person to serve as vice president of the United States.

Harris was also the second African American woman and the first South Asian American to serve in the U.S. Senate. She is the first HBCU graduate to be vice president.

Harris is a member of Alpha Kappa Alpha Sorority. The sorority was founded at Harris's alma mater, Howard University, in 1908. It was the first Black sorority. Its mission is to "cultivate and encourage high scholastic and ethical standards, to promote unity and friendship among college women, to study and help alleviate problems concerning girls and women in order to improve their social stature, to maintain a progressive interest in college life, and to be of 'Service to All Mankind.'"

Harris believes that attending an HBCU helped to prepare her for the success that she has had as an adult.

Boseman died in 2020 after a battle with cancer. Howard University named their College of Fine Arts after him in 2021.

Chadwick Boseman attended Howard University and graduated in 2000 with a degree in fine arts. After he graduated from college, he attended a summer program in London. He moved to Los Angeles in 2008 to become an actor.

Chadwick Boseman played a lot of characters in movies. He also played real-life people including Jackie Robinson, James Brown, and Thurgood Marshall. His most famous role was that of King T'Challa/Black Panther in the movie *Black Panther*. This movie was very successful at the box office and won multiple awards.

Boseman was the graduation speaker at Howard University in 2018. He talked about the importance of HBCUs and about how Howard gave him a sense of pride that impacted the kinds of roles he wanted to play. He wanted to act in movies that brought pride to the Black community. He remained true to that throughout his life and refused to play roles that portrayed Black people as stereotypes.

CHAPTER 4

HBCUs Today

HBCUs are located in 19 states, plus Washington, D.C., and the U.S. Virgin Islands. HBCUs were built to provide a way for Black students to go to college, but many students of different backgrounds attend HBCUs today.

In 2008, Joshua Packwood made history by being the first White **valedictorian** of an HBCU. He graduated from Morehouse College in Atlanta, Georgia. Packwood had a tough childhood. He moved in with his Black childhood friend during middle school. He felt like a member of the family and wanted to have that feeling in college, so he chose an HBCU.

HBCUs have been serving students in the United States for nearly 200 years.

Einstein was best known for developing the theory of relativity.
He received the Nobel Prize for Physics in 1921.

HBCUs have always welcomed people of all races and backgrounds. In 1946 Albert Einstein, who was Jewish and an activist for social justice, taught classes at Lincoln University in Pennsylvania. Lincoln was the first HBCU that gave out degrees. Einstein believed that the way Black people were treated in the United States was wrong. As a way to thank Einstein, Lincoln University gave him an honorary degree during his visit.

Many professors and students teach at and attend HBCUs. They like being a part of HBCUs for the family atmosphere, diversity, and the supportive culture. At some HBCUs, the number of White students far exceeds Black students.

After the murder of George Floyd in May 2020, people protested all over the United States. They even protested in other countries too. The protests in the summer of 2020 were the largest protests in history.

Many students decided to apply to HBCUs after protesting in the summer of 2020. They wanted to feel welcomed and accepted. Morgan State University, North Carolina A&T State University, Spelman College, and Howard University all had a large number of students apply in 2020.

In 2020, every single state in America saw large protests against the treatment of Black people.

HBCUs are an important part of our history! They started because of a dark era in our past but have provided a path to success for many students who wouldn't have been able to attend college otherwise.

College fairs bring representatives from colleges and universities all across America to you. They are a great way to learn more about opportunities at HBCUs!

Making a Way Out of NO WAY!!!

Journaling Your Way to Justice!

Have you ever heard of a vision board? People create vision boards to set goals for their future. You can do the same thing by creating a Justice Journal! In your Justice Journal, you can write your way to a better future for everyone.

Start by taking a notebook and adding things to the cover that represent the kind of world you want to see. You can use magazine clippings, crayons, markers, colored pencils, or words. Just be creative in designing your Justice Journal. It's a place where you will write about the world you want to see and then make a plan to create it!

As we have learned in this book, HBCUs exist because people refused to accept that college and universities were not a place for them. Because someone saw a need and did something about it, it created a way out of what people thought was no way.

Identify something in your school, community, or neighborhood that might be taking away or denying something from someone else. What can you do about it? How can you make a way out of no way?

Write or draw in your Justice Journal and create a plan to identify the problem, form possible solutions, and involve others in the plan to make a change!

EXTEND YOUR LEARNING

Tyree, Tia C. M., and Christopher D. Cathcart, eds. *HBCU Experience—The Book: A Collection of Essays Celebrating the Black College Experience*. Xlibris, 2014.

GLOSSARY

abolished (uh-BAH-lishd) formally put an end to a system, practice, or institution

abolitionists (ah-bah-LIH-shuh-nistz) people who supported the outlawing of slavery

activist (AK-tih-vist) a person who campaigns to bring about political or social change

anti-literacy laws (ahn-TYE-lih-tuh-ruh-see LAWZ) extensions of the slave code system, preventing the enslaved Black population from learning how to read or write

culture (KUL-chuhr) the customs, arts, social institutions, and achievements of a particular nation, people, or other social group

diversity (duh-VER-suh-tee) the practice of including or involving people from a range of different social and ethnic backgrounds and of different genders and sexual orientations

fraternities (fruh-TUHR-nuh-teez) societies for male students in a university or college, typically for social purposes

honorary (AW-nuh-RAHR-ee) conferred as an honor, without the usual requirements or functions

literate (LIH-tuh-ruht) able to read and write

nonviolence (nahn-VYE-uh-luhnss) the use of peaceful means, not force, to bring about political or social change

scholarship (SKAH-luhr-ship) money given to a student to pay for education costs

social justice (SOH-shuhl JUH-stuhss) the relation of balance between individuals and society measured by comparing distribution of wealth differences, from personal liberties to fair privilege opportunities

sororities (suh-ROHR-uh-teez) societies for female students in a university or college, typically for social purposes

stereotypes (STEHR-ee-uh-typz) widely held but fixed and oversimplified images or ideas of a particular type of person or thing

valedictorian (vah-luh-dik-TOHR-ee-uhn) a student, typically having the highest academic achievements of the class, who delivers the valedictory speech at a graduation ceremony

INDEX